Tim Dowling was born in Connecticut in 1963. As a features writer and columnist he has written for the *Guardian*, *Daily Telegraph Magazine*, the *Sunday Telegraph*, the *Independent on Sunday*, the *Spectator*, *GQ* and various other magazines. He lives in London with his wife and three sons. He is the author of *The Inventor of Disposable Culture: King Camp Gillette*.

Knife and Packer are best known for the popular long-running cartoon strip 'It's Grim Up North London' in *Private Eye*. Their cartoon strips also appear regularly in the *Sunday Times* and the *Guardian*. They have also written and illustrated two children's books.

NOT THE ARCHER

PRISON DIARY

BY JA 8008

NOT THE ARCHER

PRISON

DIARY

BY JA 8008

AS TOLD TO TIM DOWLING

CARTOONS BY KNIFE AND PACKER

EBURY
PRESS

1 3 5 7 9 10 8 6 4 2

First published 2002 by Ebury Press,
An imprint of Random House,
20 Vauxhall Bridge Road, London SW1V 2SA
www.randomhouse.co.uk

Random House Australia (Pty) Limited
20 Alfred Street, Milsons Point, Sydney,
New South Wales 2061, Australia

Random House New Zealand Limited
18 Poland Road, Glenfield, Auckland 10, New Zealand

Random House South Africa (Pty) Limited
Endulini, 5a Jubilee Road, Parktown 2193, South Africa

The Random House Group Limited Reg. No. 954009

www.randomhouse.co.uk

Printed and bound in Great Britain
by Bookmarque Limited, Croydon, Surrey

A CIP catalogue record for this book
is available from the British Library.

Cover designed by the Senate
Interior by seagulls

ISBN 0 09189 239 2

DAY 1

2:07 PM

'I sentence you to four years,' says the judge, his hoarse voice thick with bias. Normally when this happens, it is my signal to face the audience to receive a thunderous standing ovation, but this is no ordinary packed matinee performance of my hit play *The Accused*. This is a real life courtroom drama, and only a few people are clapping. The judge orders me to be taken down to the cells.

An overweight security guard leads me downstairs, into the bowels of the building and down a dark, dank, magnolia-coloured corridor. At the end of this bleak, beige 'hellway' is a large steel door, which my companion unlocks with a key. I estimate the door to be approximately seven feet high and three and a half feet wide, as I am 5'11" and a trim 175 pounds and I fit through with ease. We approach a court official, who could also afford to skip a few meals, seated at a small desk. Then the cruel, pitiless form filling begins.

'Name?'

'Archer'

'Age?'

'61.'

'Weight?'

'170 pounds'

'What's that in kilograms?' I tell him I have never used kilograms in my life and don't intend to start now. He breaks into a broad, overweight grin.

Then the first 'screw' returns and takes me to a small room, ten feet by three feet, nothing but four bare walls, a ceiling, a narrow bench and a floor. He ushers me inside before departing. When he is finally gone and I dare to approach the large, cold steel door, my worst suspicions are immediately confirmed. I am locked in.

2:53 PM

After almost a quarter of an hour of being 'banged up', I am allowed out to speak briefly with my 'brief', who has come to brief me on what is to happen next. Nick, who is not only my QC but also my best friend in the world, confirms that I am in custody, and that under the circumstances it is extremely unlikely that I will be allowed to keep my 8:30 table at Le Caprice. He tells me that I am to be sent to Hellmarsh, Britain's worst ever jail, renowned for its bad food and loud noises. I put on a brave face, but when my QC leaves I feel the first tinges of apprehension. I now believe this is going to be my most difficult undercover assignment yet.

3:10 PM

I am sent back to my cell, which is still bare, with no clock or recent magazines. There is nothing to do but stare at the graffiti desecrating the four flesh-toned walls: 'This sucks'; 'Kill All Judges' (one concedes the point) and 'Kevin Jones is inocent'.[1] I pass the time by counting my heartbeats out loud, which is probably the only thing that keeps me sane. It is not long before I am well past 500. And as I keep myself fit with daily sessions in my own private gym, my heart rate is rarely more than 62 beats per minute. You do the maths.

The burly guard finally reappears, opens the door and escorts me back down the same bleak peach-coloured corridor. Already I feel myself settling into prison's dull, dispiriting routine. The burly guard

---

1. Many prisoners, sadly, can not spell.

motions to his beefy colleague, who takes away my money and the £900 Montblanc Solitaire fountain pen given to me by Gandhi, who, I suddenly recall, was also wrongly imprisoned for his beliefs. The officer holds the pen in his fleshy fingers and eyes it suspiciously. 'I have a receipt for that at home,' I say, risking a knowing smirk.[2] But the beefy guard does not return my smirk. Instead he handcuffs me to an immense female officer who in turn leads me to a white, thickly set van. Flashbulbs explode as we exit the underground car park. As the van winds through the rain-wetted streets of London, I glimpse an *Evening Standard* placard, which has already been updated with the latest bombshell: ARCHER SENT TO JAIL. The clear implication, that I was wrongly convicted in a stunning instance of grotesque injustice, is obvious from the outraged handwriting. I am grateful for the support, and manage a smile for the first time in many minutes.

After what seems an eternity, the van turns down a side street past yet another phalanx of press photographers, and I get my first glimpse of what is to be my

---

2. This is true. Gandhi gave me the receipt, in case I didn't like the colour.

new residence. Hellmarsh certainly lives up to its name, and by that I do not mean that it is a marsh, although it is in a low, marshy area. I mean that it is like Hell in prison form.

5:49 PM

Once inside the prison I am taken to a waiting area, where I wait. 'Archer!' calls a gruff voice. I enter another room. By now I am used to the soul-destroying routine. 'Name, age, height, weight,' the officer demands.

'Archer, 59, 6 ft 1, 165 lbs.'

Then I am told to take off all my clothes. The officer reads out the labels as I go: 'Aquascutum, Hilditch & Key, YSL, Church's, Speedo...is this a swimming costume, Archer?'

'It is,' I reply. As a precaution I had worn my trunks under my clothes, in the event that the prison swimming pool lacked suitable changing facilities. I had hoped for an acquittal, of course, but it made sense to go to court prepared for the worst.

6:12 PM

I am escorted to the medical wing, where once again I
am kept waiting.

'The doctor will see you now,' says the desk officer, finally. The young prison GP seems nervous and
apologetic, but I assure him that he is only doing his
job. He pulls out a sheaf of forms – more forms! – and
I settle in for the by now almost comforting routine.

'Do you smoke?'

'No'

'Drink?'

'No. Unless Krug counts. It's a champagne. The
world's finest, in my opinion.'

'Drugs?'

'Never.'

'Any history of mental illness?'

'Absolutely not.'

'Have you ever tried to abuse yourself?'

'I'm sorry, Doctor, but I consider that to be a private matter.' I am determined to keep my dignity.

6:51 PM

After another seemingly endless wait, I am at last escorted to my cell. It measures just three paces by five. There is a small, hard bed made up with mismatched, clashing sheets. Contrary to what people might imagine are the 'cushy' conditions in Britain's prisons today, the cell has no television, no curtains, no minibar. With the gravest of expectations I pull down the blanket to inspect the pillow. No mint. Apart from a chair and a narrow metal table, there is nothing but a toilet and a small sink, both with considerable lime-scale build up. From my bed the toilet is so close that without getting up I can see that the loo roll is single ply. It suddenly occurs to me that inside these walls it no longer matters that I am Lord Archer, bestselling author and former[3] Tory leader.[4] In here I'm just plain old Lord JA 8008.[5]

---

3. I added the 'former' at the insistence of my publishers, in case people might think I was still leader.

4. My publishers have also asked me to point out that when I say Conservative leader, I mean Conservative party chairman, a technical difference of little interest to the layman, perhaps, but I am happy to oblige.

5. A little later they asked me to point out that by 'chairman' I of course meant deputy chairman. Do they think my readers are fools?

8:00 PM

Soon after my arrival I am visited by John[6] the Listener. Listeners, he tells me, are 'cons' – prisoners – who have been trained to help their fellow cons by listening to them, or providing them with certain items. John tells me he has been at Hellmarsh for four years after he was caught robbing a post office and became a Listener 18 months ago, although evidently not a very good one because after nearly five minutes I'm still the one doing all the listening. He concludes his soliloquy by asking if there is anything I need. Touched at finding such genuine kindness in this otherwise harsh and uncaring environment, I thank him and ask for some bottled water, a pad of unlined A4 paper and some pens, a packet of biscuits (McVities dark chocolate, NOT milk), a razor, an extra pillow, a soft-bristled toothbrush, dental floss, a radio and some shoe trees. He says he'll see what he can do. Already I feel I have made a friend for life.

---

6. I have changed some of the names to protect the anonymity of inmates. Not this one, though.

8:45 PM

John returns with only the A4 pad and a single pen, plus a toothbrush and an extra pillow. I do not allow my disappointment to show. Instead I thank him, and gently let him know that I expect to be more impressed tomorrow. If I've learned anything in life, it's how to motivate people.

10:29 PM

I lay down on the cold, hard mattresses. I hear distant, echoing shrieks and screams, a whistle being blown, more shouting. It sounds as if the swimming pool is closing for the evening. I am too tired to think about that now. I close my eyes and sleep the sleep of the innocent, although not very well.

DAY 2

6:55 AM

By the time the sunlight filters through my little barred window I have been writing for more than three hours. Seized by the realisation that keeping a detailed prison diary might be the only salvation that could save me in this hellhole, I leapt from my uncomfortable bed, sat down on my hard, pitiless chair and wrote steadily until the guard came to escort me to breakfast, by which time I had amassed an estimated 4,362 words. In fact by then I had already written about breakfast, but I subsequently found the reality to be so starkly different that I was forced to throw out several pages and begin again. I'm on a very steep learning curve.

'Breakfast' is served on the lowest landing, which for me, with my cell on one of the higher landings, is approached by some stairs. A queue of 'lags' forms behind a set of steam trays, which ingeniously keep the food warm using some form of sub-tray in which water is heated by electricity. By the time I arrive at the front of the queue, there do not appear to be any croissants left.

'Well if it isn't his lordship,' says the con behind the

counter, 'And how the fuck[7] are we this fine morning?'

'Very well, thank you,' I reply, fixing this hardened criminal with a steady, piercing gaze. 'What would you recommend?'

'Why not try the fucking eggs? Or how about a nice fucking piece of fucking toast?'

Now you listen here, reader: I have had toast at Claridge's, toast at the Ivy and French toast at the Ritz in Paris. I have enjoyed wholewheat toast with the Beatles backstage at the Hollywood Bowl, and I had my first slice of rye toast on the maiden voyage of the *QEII*. Once, in an emergency, I even made toast myself, by heating up some sliced bread in a toaster. I consider myself to be the world's foremost expert on toast, but I have never in all my life tasted anything as unspeakable as prison toast. I cannot even begin to describe it. It is not even 'toasted' to the same degree on both sides. I return to my cell fortified with nothing more than a cup of hot water and two Kit Kats.

---

7. Prisoners say 'fuck' rather a lot. I do not wish to shock my regular readers unduly, so I will only report the saying of the word 'fuck' when I feel it is essential to the story.

9:30 AM

When I get back to my cell I find the Prison Governor, Ms Gregory, waiting for me, although I barely notice her at first, because she is a small, slightly squat woman who looks quite insignificant alongside the pile of letters and packages which have been delivered in my absence. She is, however, a smart and professional lady, wholly able to keep her obvious attraction for me in check as she explains what is to happen to me in the coming weeks. First she tells me that as a D-cat[8] prisoner I will be transferred to an open facility as soon as possible, but in the meantime she would like to move me to a shared cell with another prisoner who might benefit from my experience in the system. She asks if she can do anything else for me before then. Ignoring her sly smile, I chastely request a copy of *Roget's Thesaurus*, a book which I have always found to be absolutely necessitous, not to mention requisite, to have at my elbow when I am writing.

I spend an hour reading through my letters. I am

---

8. Prisoners are divided into four categories, A, B, C and D, with A being the most likely to escape and re-offend. D-cat includes prisoners whom the governor believes to be innocent, or those on undercover assignments. I qualify on both counts.

slightly taken aback by how supportive they are. Virtually every letter protests the way I have been treated by our corrupt legal system, and most express outrage at the length of my sentence. I am particularly moved by one which is written entirely in blood; not many people would go to such lengths to thank a humble bestselling author whose work has touched them deeply. Before I can settle down to write a suitable reply (I hope you don't mind ordinary blue biro, Mr D. Hobson of Worksop!), my cell door swings open. It is time for exercise.

11:00 AM

Exercise.

In the parched, dusty exercise yard I run into my friend from breakfast, who I discover is called Daryl (murder, says fuck a lot). He introduces me to a few of the other men from our block: Mazzer (VAT fraud, born without incisors), Tam (GBH, loved *First Among Equals*) and Big Ben (murder, dandruff). As we walk slowly along the perimeter wall, I am questioned closely as to how I'm settling in. 'How are you finding the accommodations, your fucking lordship?' asks Daryl. I am about to tell him that I'm finding them a bit cramped compared to my luxury penthouse overlooking the Thames, and he is about to laugh heartily, when we are approached by a younger con, who to my surprise immediately offers to sell me a 'gram' of 'cocaine'. 'I have never taken a drug in my life,' I tell him sternly, looking him squarely in the chest, 'and I'll thank you not to use the metric system in my presence.' The young con becomes angry and begins shouting but my 'crew', as I have already come to think of them, quickly close ranks around me. In the end I am saved by the bell, which signals that Exercise is over.

11:45 AM

I barely have time to write three pages before the 'dinner' bell sounds for lunch.[9] Interruptions, interruptions! The door swings open and I am led down. The food on offer is so unspeakable that I wouldn't wish it on my worst enemy's most disobedient dog. I fear you

---

9. Lunch is known as 'dinner' here, while supper is called 'tea'. It's taking me a bit of time to get used to all this jailhouse slang.

would begin to vomit uncontrollably if I even tried to describe it. Instead I use my prison canteen allocation to buy a bottle of water and a few small snacks, including a packet of crisps which taste almost uncannily of prawn cocktail, while still somehow continuing to taste of crisps. Odd to find such innovation in a place like this, but I've already come to expect the unexpected from Hellmarsh.

I return to my cell to find a fresh pile of supportive letters, along with the copy of *Roget's Thesaurus* I requested from the governor. It is an old and dog-eared volume, but the sight of it fills me with beatitude. I immediately sit down at my little desk and commence retorting to my bevy of missives.

12:22 PM

John the Listener drops by with a few things: some soap, a razor, a plastic bowl, a battery powered radio, some shampoo and conditioner, a bottle of Highland Spring water and two boxes of Cup a Soup (mushroom and cream of chicken). I thank this kind man profusely, while pointing out that I hadn't asked for the Cup a

Soup and I was still missing my biscuits. I added that the toothbrush he had given me the night before was medium bristled when I had clearly requested soft.

I could see that he was upset by my criticism, so I quickly set him a new challenge: I ask him to see if he can lay his hands on a small box of Maldon sea salt. The salt in this place is woefully below par. I suspect it may be iodised.

4:00 PM

The now familiar turning of the guard's key in the door's lock alerts me to the fact that it is time for 'Association', a daily one-hour period of inter-convict socialising, to which I am invited. When I walk into the recreation room I notice that a little table has been set up, and that next to it there is a huge queue of inmates waiting for me to sign copies of my many books. Without a word I take my chair and begin. First in the queue is my old friend Daryl (murder, fuck-saying) who wants me to sign 54 paperback copies of *Not A Penny More, Not A Penny Less*[10] for his girlfriend.

---

10. My first novel, available at all fine book shops.

While I get on with the task I ponder how much a signed Jeffrey Archer bestseller might be worth as prison currency. I have no idea. A few dozen Cuban cigars, perhaps? A guard's uniform and badge, along with a false passport and a plane ticket to Mexico?

Eventually a large West Indian with a huge gold earring[11] slides a hardcover volume across the desk and says, 'Sign.' I look down at the book.

'Under most circumstances, I'd be only too happy to oblige you,' I say, 'but there is a small problem. You see, I didn't write this book.' Normally I am not so fastidious about such mistakes at book signings, as I hate to disappoint punters. I've been known to sign Martin Amis's name in my time, as well as those of Stephen Hawking, Andrew Motion, Gary Rhodes and L Ron Hubbard. But this is different. 'This is an unauthorised biography of me by someone called Michael Crick,' I tell him. 'It is a book I thoroughly despise. I have never signed a copy of it in my life and I don't intend to start now.' The West Indian and I share what I shall call a frank and full exchange of views, which

---

11. Many prison inmates wear earrings, and not all of them are gay. Another lazy preconception shattered.

ends with me writing 'To Sarah, all the best, love Jeffrey,' on the flyleaf. Another friend for life?

When the queue for signings finally diminishes, I join a queue of my own, the queue for the phones, clutching my phone card[12] in my hand as I wait. When my turn finally comes I dial in great haste, knowing Association has just a few more minutes left to run. After more than 48 hours in prison it is good to hear my dear wife Mary's warm, sweet voice again. I leave a message after the beep. A bell sounds. Association is over.

As I am led back to my cell, I notice that some fresh graffiti has been scratched on the outside of my cell door in my absence. Although I glimpse it for just a fraction of a second before the heavy door slams shut and I am locked in for the next 16 hours, I don't think I will ever forget what it says:

ARCHER YOU CNUT

---

12. Because prisoners are not allowed to carry large quantities of loose change, which could easily be melted down into a gun, they pay for phone calls using ingenious plastic cards on which talking time is stored in the form of 'units'.

Stunned, I sink down onto the spare, unforgiving mattress and consider the analogy. How apt it is. Like the legendary King Cnut, I too am trying to hold back the tide, the tide of injustice, not to mention the waves of anger and bitterness that constantly threaten to swamp me here. Thinking about it, I suppose I've been a Cnut all my life, always fighting gamely against unstoppable tides. Will I, like he, finally succeed?

DAY 3

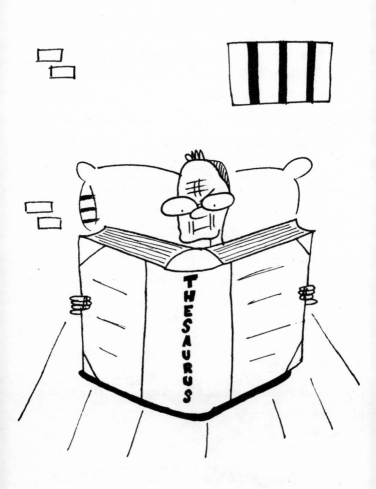

5:53 AM

A sleepless night. With *Roget's Thesaurus* as my only book, I had little to occupy my thoughts as I lay on my meagre, frangible mattress. Indeed I was grateful for the first grey shafts of dawn filtering through my little barred window. After a brisk two-hour writing session, the guard unlocks my cell and escorts me to the showers. For those readers who have never had the pleasure of using one, I should tell you that a prison shower is activated by a push button which automatically turns off the water after just a few seconds.[13] A shower lasting 35 minutes requires one to push the button no less than 70 times! I soon get the hang of it however, and leave feeling cleaner than I have in a day.

9:15 AM

Breakfast is a bowl of Corn Flakes in UHT milk. I have to fight to keep down each mouthful.

---

13. It occurs to me that many of the clever inventions designed specifically for prisons might well have applications on the outside. Note: contact a patent lawyer.

11:27 AM

The small slot in my cell door slides open unfeelingly. I am told I will be moved to my new cell in 15 minutes. Quietly I gather up my few possessions and my many letters and sit down to wait. 20 minutes later I am still waiting. Time, I think, for a Kit Kat. Delicious.

11:59 AM

The guard finally reappears. I follow him up the corridor, down a flight of stairs, down another corridor, where cheers greet me as I walk by the occupied cells of my new wing. We stop at a random steel door, which is opened to reveal a stark cell, slightly larger than my previous one, dominated by a bunk bed which is already overflowing with card and letters from well-wishers. My new cellmate, Davy, is sitting on the top bunk staring down at the pile with obvious envy.

Davy (going equipped, filthy fingernails) is a bright and talkative young man of 19, who clasps my hand warmly and before very long is telling me how much he enjoyed reading *Silence of the Lambs*. Such authorial mix-ups are not as uncommon as you might think, but I have no wish to make Davy feel ill at ease on our first meeting.

'Thank you,' I say.

'For what?' he asks.

Suddenly the bell sounds. Can it be lunchtime already? It's all 'go' in prison.

12:30 PM

Over lunch I hear a good deal of Davy's life story, of which more later. He tells me he has nearly completed his sentence, and is due to leave Hellmarsh shortly. I briefly sketch out my own life story in exchange – athletic triumph, political success, literary fame, very big house, untold riches, top secret assignment – which keeps us occupied nearly until supper time. I like Davy very much. It's good to have someone to talk to.

DAY 4

7:45 AM

I am woken from a sound sleep by the ear-splitting, aggressive throb of gangster rap music reverberating relentlessly in my skull. I certainly don't need to open my eyes in order to recall that I am 'banged up' in Hellmarsh.

'What in God's name is that infernal racket?' I shout, before I have even quite come to.

'I think it's the Sugababes,' says Davy, peering down at me from the upper bunk. 'I hope you don't mind me putting on Radio 1. Me mum always listens to it in the mornings.' If parents are playing this sort of music to their children, is it any wonder they end up in prison? What is Britain coming to?

I explain to Davy that I write most mornings, and that I intended to listen to Test Match Special on Radio 4 Long Wave in the afternoon; I would there-fore be grateful if he didn't speak to me for the next seven and a half hours. I also tell him in no uncertain terms what I think of the so-called 'Sugababes' and their irresponsible advocacy of hard drugs and cop killing. Davy says that he is working on some writing himself and understands the need for quiet, but I dare say if he really knew anything about self-discipline he wouldn't be in prison.

11:00 AM

Exercise. To stay in shape I lead Davy and Daryl through a basic aerobic workout. 'We'll begin with a very short stretch,' I tell them. 'I don't expect either of you would care to do a long stretch here in Hellmarsh, eh?' This remark is greeted by an awkward silence. I am learning there are some things one just doesn't joke about inside.

2:10 PM

After a quiet lunch in my cell (more prawn flavoured crisps, two Kit Kats, an apple, a dish of prison-issue ice cream and a tantalising orange-flavoured concoction known inside as 'Tango'), I settle down for a bit more writing, with every intention of exposing the gross malignancy which lies at the dark heart of Britain's prison system, while catching up with events at the Oval via Radio 4.

After just a few days in Hellmarsh, I have learned some uncomfortable truths about prison life: it is very, very uncomfortable. I think all the so-called 'lock-'em-up-and-throw-away-the-key' types in the Conservative party would be fairly surprised to see a peer of the realm and a loyal Tory – a member in good standing of the MCC no less – 'banged up' for up to 15 hours a day in the company of a man who tried to break into a leisure centre. Is this what passes for rehabilitation in this country? Shall we continue to let offenders leave jail worse off than they went in? Is it not time that we should be led by compassion and common sense, rather than blind revenge? Who breaks a butterfly like myself upon a wheel like Hellmarsh?

Five minutes before the tea interval, Thorpe makes a pathetic stab at a full toss and is out for all of 14. He should be taken out and shot.

DAY 5

5:59 AM

My arduous prison routine is now very similar to the arduous routine I stick to when I'm ensconced in my penthouse in Alembic House: as soon as the first shafts of dawn light filter through my little barred window, I rise and begin my initial two-hour writing burst of the day. Davy sleeps soundly throughout.

Because today is Sunday, breakfast is a larger affair: eggs, beans, chips, Kit Kat, half a bag of Cheesy Wotsits. Afterwards I elect to attend C of E chapel services. Although I am not particularly religious, I do enjoy going to church and meeting fans. Here in Hellmarsh, it's also a chance to leave my cramped cell for a whole precious hour.

All in all about 25 inmates attend the service, which is held in a room not quite as spacious as I'd hoped. After a few hymns, the vicar, dressed in a greasy jacket and shabby dog-collar, announces that the subject of the sermon will be the story of Kane and Abel. He looks directly at me as he says this, with a knowing wink which I take as a cue to stand up and outline the timeless story of two rich and powerful men, one from a distinguished Boston banking family, the other a Polish immigrant who ruthlessly clawed his way out of poverty.[14] I am not quite able to finish the story by the time the bell cruelly signals the end of the hour, but I fancy most of my audience knew it well enough anyway. I thank the greasy vicar, shake his limp hand and return to my wing with the others.

2:40 PM

After lunch Davy continues to pour his heart out to me, telling me about the unspeakable boredom of his half-term holiday which drove him to attempt to break into the local leisure centre with some friends. If you told me one week ago that I would be chatting about the finer points of breaking into a leisure centre while sharing my last Kit Kat with a career criminal, I would have hit you. But here I am.

---

14. *St Louis Post-Despatch* called it 'a masterpiece of narrative craftsmanship'.

4:20 PM

India 178 without loss. I know now the true meaning of the word despair.

DAY 6

5:52 AM

Wake to find the sunlight already filtering through my little barred window. I write undisturbed until 8:00, when Davy wakes up and starts peppering me with questions. He asks me if I will look at the story he is working on when he is finished. I agree to give him an honest opinion, but he says he is most worried about his poor spelling.

'Good writing is about plot and storytelling,' I tell him, 'not spelling and character development.' I tell him of my hero Oscar Wilde, who once wrote an entire poem about prison in which he misspelled jail every single time. If you can get away with that, you can get away with anything! Clearly impressed, Davy asks me about my other literary heroes.

'I think I will be the world's finest living writer,' I say, 'when I manage to combine the storytelling ability of Rudyard Kipling, the descriptive powers of Charles Dickens and the clean, direct prose style of Nick Faldo.' Perhaps with this diary I will finally achieve all three.

9:30 AM

Light breakfast (half a mug of Highland Spring, 12 Smarties).

12:45 PM

Lunch (Heinz 'Bill & Ben' Pasta Shapes with mini sausages in tomato sauce, Kit Kat, crisps).

3:23 PM

The governor, Ms Gregory, comes by unannounced, to speak to me about Education. Since it looks like I will be 'banged up' in Hellmarsh for at least a fortnight, she wishes to know if I am interested in taking any classes while I'm here. I'm flattered. I've always enjoyed teaching. I inquire about creative writing courses.

'Yes, we do have one,' she says, wearily. I can tell from the tone of her voice that she is unhappy with the present instructor.

'Well, you are no doubt aware that I fancy myself a bit of a writer,' I say with comic modesty.

'I'm sorry, but I'm afraid I've never read any of your books,' she says. People often tell me that they have never read my books, perhaps because they are embarrassed, although it is always glaringly obvious to me that they are lying. Given my overall sales figures, it is quite simply statistically impossible. I have worked out that everyone in Britain has read at least two, which is more than you can say for Mr William G Shakespeare.

'In that case,' I reply, 'I'm working on something at the moment which you may be interested in.' I hand her the latest pages of my prison diary. She peruses the first few pages intently.

'Actually, I think our creative writing class would do you a lot of good,' she says.

'Splendid. When do I start?'

'I can sign you up this week. It's on Friday afternoons. Guard!'

At last, I think, a chance to do something worthwhile in this hellhole.

6:45 PM

Association. I enjoy a little television with Davy (going equipped, cellmate) and Ron, who says he is in for burglary and aggravated assault. He asks me what I'm in for, though he knows full well, or at least he thinks he does. My QC Nick advised me not to discuss the details of my case with anyone while in prison, so I simply tell him I am here largely because I have been betrayed by one of my closest friends in the world, and also by a former secretary, who at the time was not only my secretary but also one of my closest friends in the world. Ron smiles and says he can easily arrange to have them both killed if I wish. I don't doubt it for a minute. Remembering my lawyer's advice, I have decided against recording my reply here.

Ron shows me his copy of the *Sun*, a paper which I have never read before. I see that Emma Nicholson MP is accusing me of mismanaging funds which I raised to help the Kurds. Now there's someone I wouldn't mind getting rid of.

DAY 7

7:32 AM

Blast. I've overslept again. The first rays of sunlight have long since begun filtering through my little barred window. An hour's valuable writing time is now lost forever.

8:45 AM

Shower. Running out of conditioner. Skip breakfast in order to write. Just a quick Kit Kat and some pretzels and three biscuits (McVities, of course!).

11:00 AM

Another huge postbag arrives. Nearly 100 letters of unqualified support, plus a parcel of food & clothing from Mary's PA, who is not just Mary's PA but also one of Mary's closest friends. She remembered the sweater with the reindeers on it, the one Gyles Brandreth gave me. What would I do without my loving wife and her loyal support staff?

12:10 PM

Lunch is something called 'vegetarian bake' which is, if you can believe it, the designated 'healthy option' on today's menu. Merely smelling it makes me feel sick. I make my own arrangements at the canteen and take lunch in my cell (Pringles, Kit Kat, Ribena, M&Ms, Twiglets). I worry about losing more weight. I am, according to the prison scales, now down to 180 pounds.

2:15 PM

Workshop.

Most prisoners in Hellmarsh work in return for a small addition to their weekly allowance (£12.50 per week, less than one ten-thousandth of my income on the outside, if I've done my figures right). Today I supplement my wage by packing breakfast bags for another prison. I'm in charge of adding the little packets of sugar. It's demanding work made slightly more pleasant by the company. I work with a con from another wing, whom I'll call Paddy, because he is Irish. What is it about the music of a sweet, lilting

Irish accent that makes it almost impossible for me to understand a single word?

'Begora,' Paddy began, before recounting to me his entire life story in that unmistakable colourful Celtic gibberish. From what of it I understood, I gather that on the 'outside' Paddy was a common labourer, always ready with a smile and a joke but rather too fond of a drink, who because of his natural idleness fell in with a bad crowd of other Irishmen. Together they hatched an elaborate plot to obtain money by deception which fell apart because of their own stupidity. Sadly it's a tale I feel I've heard too many times before, but he tells it so well I can't help laughing at his misfortune. God bless the Irish!

'Keep up with the sugar, Archer,' snaps the guard. And so we fall silent, and go back to work.

Next I strike up a conversation with the man to my left, Bob the Drug Dealer (drug dealing). Normally I abhor drugs and have long thought that those caught dealing them should receive the death penalty, but Bob is such a warm and likeable chap that I'm not even sure I believe in the death penalty any more. In any case I am spellbound by his explanation of the way drug-trafficking works in prison. This is what I've come to prison for, after all: to learn, so that in future my precisely detailed thrillers will be even more accurate, and will lead to widespread prison reforms which will almost certainly be named after me. In short, I want to give something back.

According to Bob drugs can be smuggled inside in all sorts of ingenious ways; through visitors, in food, even hidden in the spines of books donated to the prison library! I'm so fascinated by this information that I fall behind on the assembly line once again.

'We'll just hide the evidence, Jeff,' says Bob, as he proceeds to shove packet after packet of sugar down the front of my shirt before the guard can see. It's amazing how people look out for you in prison. Who says there is no such thing as *Honour Among Thieves*[15]?

---

15. 'The best thriller I've read in years' – Jonathan King, *Smash Hits*.

5:25 PM

Supper (Cup a Soup (cream of chicken (lovely!)), packet of wine gums, Kinder egg).

6:00 PM

I decide to stay in my cell during Association to make a start on my swollen postbag, but I'm constantly interrupted by an endless stream of visitors to my cell door. To my surprise, almost all of them ask me if I have any spare sugar. I don't normally bother with sugar, so it's lucky I have my bumper supply from Workshop with Bob this afternoon. I end up giving away almost half the packets. It's amazing how little things like sugar become so important in the place like this. Some of the cons were hiding the packets in their shoes!

DAY 8

10:30 AM

Exercise. I take a brisk clockwise stroll with Davy (cell mate), when I see a knot of 'lags' loitering and murmuring under the grey, redbrick wall. 'Morning, gentlemen,' I say on approaching. 'Not plotting an escape I hope!' Surprisingly, they do not laugh. Subtly I change tack: 'Of course if you are, your secret is safe with me. I'm here at Hellmarsh as an impartial observer.'

'You know much about escapes, do you, Jeff?' asks one. Few of the inmates bother with my title any more, which suits me just fine.

'Only if flying a home-made aeroplane plane out of Colditz counts,' I reply. The cons exchange stunned glances.

'Ain't you a little too young to have been in the war?' another inquires suspiciously. I have to smile at this.

'Perhaps I just look too young. Come along, Davy.' I make a mental note to report the escape plot to my publisher straight away.

11:20 AM

The censor arrives with another huge mailbag for me, brimming with packages, letters and cards. Naturally the parcels and envelopes have already been opened. The censor cheerfully admits he simply doesn't have time to read them all, but tells me that from his brief overview it appears that supportive letters have now widened their lead over critical ones by a margin of 300 to 1. Two of the packages contain bibles. I give one to Davy, and ask what I might do with the other. I have no use for a bible myself, since I memorised the King James Version long ago. Davy suggests I donate it to the prison library. I ask if this is possible, and the censor assures me that it is. A trifling good deed perhaps, but a good deed nonetheless. I sign the bible's title page, and hand it over.

12:00 PM

I spend the time before lunch looking over my post-bag. There is a postcard from Mary (wife, fragrant), postmarked in Scotland, saying all is well. I'm glad she's getting back to her day-to-day routine. She knows I wouldn't have it any other way.

7:00 PM

During Association I tell Daryl (murder, fuck-saying), Tam (GBH, *First Among Equals*), and Graham (robbery, cheap plastic watch) about my upcoming creative writing classes, and invite them all to sign up for instruction.

'What are you gonna be teaching, like?' asks Graham, who says 'like' almost as often as Daryl says 'fuck'.

'Oh, I think we'll start with basic sentence structure,' I reply, 'although I imagine most inmates at Hellmarsh would wish to keep their sentences as short as possible!' They stare at me blankly. I sometimes wonder if there is such a thing as prison humour.

9:30 PM

I can't sleep. Somewhere on a lower floor, someone is blasting out the evil rap tirades of the Sugababes again. Although I'm not normally a religious man, at times like these I find it helps me to think of Jesus, and the amazing parallels between my life and His. It must be more than mere coincidence.

DAY 9

10:30 AM

Exercise. Davy (going equipped, cellmate), Daryl (murder, fuck), Gary (fraud, terrible posture) and I take our usual walk, while Daryl fills me in on a few of our more dangerous colleagues. Because Hellmarsh is a Category A prison, some seriously unpleasant criminals find themselves 'banged up' here.

Daryl points out a tough looking con over near the swings. 'Now that fucker,' he says, 'was the fucking leader of one major fucking drug ring.' I can't help noticing that Daryl now tones down his language in front of me. I tell him I am increasingly fascinated by the extent of the drug problem in Britain. Daryl explains how drug-traffickers often force mules to swallow up to a dozen packages containing heroin and cocaine before they come into this country.

'I know there are evil people in the world, but I can't believe anyone would do that to a defenceless mule,' I say, shaking my head. But how much longer will I be shocked by such horrors? When will these disgusting revelations become routine, even hilarious? Never, I hope.

We pass the 'Escape Committee'.

'Morning Jeff,' says their leader. 'How's the aeroplane coming on?'

'Fine thank you,' I reply. I then spot one of Hellmarsh's more famous residents, a small balding man with a neat moustache, who is busy tending a forlorn patch of geraniums. An incongruous setting perhaps, but I believe I would recognise Carlos the Jackal anywhere. 'Well, look who it is,' I say, pointing.

'That's Reg,' says Gary. 'He's from Leytonstone.'

'Of course he is,' I reply. 'And I'll wager he also has a flawless London accent to prove it.'

'Well, it's similar to mine,' answers the ever gullible Gary, 'but then we did go to the same primary school.'

'Naturally,' I say. I approach the Jackal, my 'crew' in tow. He seems surprised to see me, to say the least.

'Well, Carlos, we meet at last.'

'What?'

'Hi Reg,' adds the confused Gary meekly.

'Who is this ponce?'[16] snarls the cunning Jackal, his studied cockney twang as pitch perfect as I had imagined.

---

16. 'Ponce' is prison slang for an Oxbridge-educated person. As such (Brasenose) I would hear it a lot over the course of my stay.

'I am the man who wrote the bestsellers on whose plots you based many of your most audacious terrorist crimes,' I reply sternly, 'and I am not best pleased. If there's one thing I can't stomach, it's a plagiarist.'

In the end my crew pulled us apart before I did something which might have got me 'put on report', but we all decided it would be best if I avoided the exercise yard for a few days.

DAY 10

3:00 PM

'Damn you, Little Steve, sound it out! We're going to keep at this until you jolly well get it right! If I can teach Michael Barrymore to swim, then I can damn well teach you to read!'

My first creative writing class is well underway. I've ten days at the most to turn these hardened criminals into novelists, and I quickly discover only half of them can write their own name. Worse still, the hour began with a mix-up which wasted precious time: I arrived to find that I had mistakenly been signed up to *attend* the creative writing course, rather than teach it, and the previous instructor had not been told he was being replaced. He seemed a well-meaning chap, but when I discovered he had not one million-selling novel to his name, I soon made it clear to him who would be leading the class. It wasn't long before yours truly was at the blackboard taking Little Steve (deception, little) through the first sentence of *The Fourth Estate*,[17] and the 'professor' was sitting in the back row nervously fidgeting with the panic button all

---

17. 'Another super-great read from my favourite genius writer!!!!!!!' – Amazon.com review.

outsiders must wear when they enter Hellmarsh.

The class ended prematurely some minutes later when four guards burst in and threw me to the ground. I was then dragged away and placed in segregation. The reason for this was not quite clear at the time, and since I have been in segregation ever since it's impossible to get any more information, but I have been able to piece together a version of events. Apparently there had been a 'security breach', i.e. some lunatic had gone haywire during Education, leading to what is known as a 'lock-down' situation. I gather that the officers who threw me to the floor and stood on my neck for half an hour did so in order to protect me: as a bestselling author and high-profile Tory fundraiser I am an obvious target for any angry, stir-crazy lifer with nothing to lose. That would certainly explain why I'm now 'banged-up' in segregation. While I appreciate their concerns for my safety, I can only hope I don't have to spend too long in this cell, smaller than any I have seen yet, without company, or my precious radio, or my books, or even pen and paper: absolutely nothing. I don't even want to tell you how I'm writing this.

DAY 11

4:22 PM

At last I am back on the wing, but there is bad news from the governor's office delivered by a guard. After my 24 hours in segregation I have lost my category D status. I am for the moment a category C prisoner: mad, bad and dangerous to know. Of course I protested vociferously; it seems jolly unfair that I should suffer for a decision taken largely to protect me from other prisoners! I tell the guard I wish to appeal.

5:00 PM

In my absence the post has piled up alarmingly. The first 30 letters I open all express unqualified support. The 31st is an indecent proposal from a young lady, which I put to one side. The next 20 are, if anything, even more supportive than the first 30. I wish the judge who presided over my trial could see how many decent people think he's a complete fool.

There are also four more bibles and two copies of the New Testament in the pile. 'Good news' for the prison library.

6:15 PM

Association. Everyone seems pleased to see me back. Bob the Drug Dealer (drug dealing, sugar) shakes my hand and tells me I am doing a wonderful thing by donating all the bibles that are sent to me by well-meaning religious fanatics. I can't help but notice that he is clutching one of the new prison library bibles as he speaks. I'm glad to see something I've done is helping to turn this formerly evil man around. If my autograph on the inside cover encourages a few more cons to pick up the good book, then my research trip to prison has been worth every minute.

'Careful,' I joke, pointing to Bob's bible. 'You know what Disraeli said: "Religion is the opiate of the masses".'

'He was quite right, Jeff,' says Bob, 'quite right.'

DAY 12

6:02 AM

I wake after the strangest dream: I find myself at an informal summer drinks party at Gillian Shepherd's house, which is full of dear friends, most of whom I have not seen for a long time. My wife Mary is there, and she keeps looking at her watch, until I feel obliged to whisper that she is being extremely rude. Suddenly there is a trumpet fanfare, and Margaret Thatcher is rolled into the sitting room on casters. 'Baroness Thatcher,' I say, 'how delightful to see you.'

'Jeffrey,' she says, rising to her feet slowly, and placing a hand on Iain Duncan Smith's bowed head for support, 'your party needs you. Your country needs you. And so it is with the greatest confidence that I hereby crown you Prime Minister of Great Britain.' I begin to make my acceptance speech – the all-purpose one I keep in my wallet – but am drowned out by a persistent beeping from one of my ankles. What can it mean?

10:30 AM

As it's Sunday, I push the button inside my cell which lights the light outside my cell, in order to indicate to the guard on duty that I wish to attend chapel. Unfortunately, the guard on duty does not see my light until the C of E shift has left the wing. By the time he unlocks my door there is only one slot remaining, an Islamic prayer meeting held by a prison faith group called 'al-Muhajiroun'. Not my usual cup of religious tea, perhaps, but I am eager to stretch my legs. In any case I feel I will fit in well enough, if only because of my tireless work supporting the Kurdish people.

While I do not pretend to be more than a minor expert on Islam, I nevertheless found these men to be warm, friendly and instantly likeable. I was pleased to see that not one of them smoked. I've forgotten most of my Arabic, but I did pick up a few of their chants ('Dehth-tu Ahm-raiahka!', etc), which we shouted until we were all quite hoarse. I enjoy learning about other faiths, even those I don't believe in at all.

I listen patiently to the visiting Imam's sermon, waiting my turn to speak. When it finally comes I stand politely and say words to the effect that while I greatly appreciate and respect the Imam's beliefs, I believe him to be wholly wrong in this matter.

'History will show you that Britain's place is and

has always been alongside America. Our democracies and our beliefs are entwined. I'm sure everyone here will agree with me when I say that we should support US foreign policy aims as if they were our own.' The service ends with a sort of mini-riot, which I can only assume has some traditional significance. Once again, I am saved by the bell.

DAY 13

5:59 AM

Light filters through my little barred window. Two thousands words find their way onto my A4 pad.

9:00 AM

Breakfast (hard-boiled egg, Kit Kat, half a mug of Sunny Delight).

10:30 AM

Davy (going equipped, cellmate) is still begging me to look at his writing. Finally I relent. He proceeds to hand me, on a single page, a short poem which I record exactly here:

Sell Mate Story – D Express

> *He wake me up when it still dark out, all ways*
> > *shouting himself.*
>
> *Treat me like his servent. Sick of his shit. All ways*
> > *tellin me wot to do.*
>
> *Blastin out the radio 4 – you & yours, moneybox*
> > *live*

I even asked for tranfser but gov dont listen. Cant
stand his talkin no more. Thinks
he's Lord god all mitey. If he dont stop talking Im
gonna kill him I swear

He smells
& just eats sweets all day

I think you'll have to agree that even with the spelling mistakes, it is a powerful piece of writing. I can only imagine the hell this boy went through with his previous cellmate. I think you'll be hearing a lot from young Davy – or 'D Express' as he appears to style himself – in future. I am so impressed by the poem I offer to help him in securing a publisher, but he says he already has an agent. I'm not surprised.

2:46 PM

The governor, Ms Gregory, finds another excuse to drop by and see me. She says she wants to talk to me about my appeal.

'It's not something I'm particularly comfortable speaking about,' I say, 'but I've been told it's a sort of animal magnetism combined with a genuine love of women. I'm also a great listener, and of course I keep myself scrupulously clean.'

'I'm talking about your appeal against category C status,' she says brusquely. 'I believe you said you wished to go ahead with it.' She may sound all business, but a fire burns within her. I'm sure of it.

'You are damn well right I want to appeal. It is utterly inhuman classifying people as AA or B or C or D. I'm a human being damn it, not a battery!' At the time I was very angry. Normally I would never use a word like 'damn' in front of a lady, and if I'd known there was a rule against swearing at the governor, I certainly wouldn't have done it. I'd like to see a list of these so-called 'rules'. In the end I'm glad to be barred from Association for the day. It will give me a chance to write.

5:23 PM

Supper (2 packets crisps, sparkling water, Terry's chocolate orange, Fruit Winder). It's finally happening: I'm getting used to prison food. Soon I'll be calling it 'tea', like some sort of serial killer.

8:00 PM

I look over my diary account of the day's events. In
spite of the swearing, I'm still extremely pleased with
the battery analogy, although it occurs to me that there
are no B batteries. I make a note to write to my secretary and ask her to check that.

DAY 14

9:24 AM

A quick breakfast (two Tic Tacs and a Marathon bar, known as a 'Snickers' inside), followed by a burst of writing.

11:00 AM

Post. Support is now running more than 400 to 1. Seven more signed bibles for the prison library.

12:00 PM

I have an official visit scheduled with literary agent, who I would count not only among my many agents but also among my many closest friends. At the appointed hour I am escorted to a small room with windows on all sides, where in full view of the guards I sign contracts for two new thrillers and the earth-shattering prison diary which you are reading now, hopefully in hardcover. Now that I have secured advances for them these books will give a real purpose to my time in Hellmarsh, a reason to carry on with each solitary day. My only worry now is that I won't be in prison long enough to finish them all!

4:00 PM

Can't stop thinking about the Gillian Shepherd dream, which I've now had two nights running. It seems to be pointing me toward some kind of inevitable type of destiny. I promise myself I will not miss any opportunity to fulfil that destiny.

DAY 15

8:30 PM

A good day of writing well written, if I do say so myself. I rise at six sharp and write for two hours, covering the events of yesterday. After breakfast, I write about breakfast until lunch. Immediately following lunch I set to work detailing my more memorable lunchtime experiences. This carries me through until evening, when I have a frugal supper. After dashing off a few pages on the subject of supper I find myself too exhausted to write about post-supper events, so I put myself to bed as soon as I finish the sentence I am writing right now.

DAY 16

4:00 PM

Association. I wander over to the television area and sit next to a man of about my age, 57, although obviously much less trim, or I would have certainly mistaken him for someone much younger, as people often do with me. The afternoon movie is *Brubaker*, starring Robert Redford. It's about a reform-minded prison governor who goes undercover as an inmate in order to expose the harsh realities of life 'inside'. In style and structure it is remarkably similar to my own upcoming thriller, *Escape From Hellmarsh*, although I note that Robert Redford would be a bit too old to play me now. I introduce myself to the gentleman sitting next to me, who is called Michael. I end up telling him how the film ends so we can concentrate on our conversation.

Michael, I soon discover, was until recently a successful chief financial officer in a leading software firm. He tells me he's serving a four-year sentence for insider trading.

'Insider trading? Tell me how that works,' I reply.

'Well, Jeff, I was accused of tipping off my family and friends that my company, in which they had invested heavily, was about to go bust due to serious accounting irregularities. This enabled them to sell their stock and keep the profits they'd earned thanks to the company's hugely inflated share price.' I was, to say the least, shocked.

'Hold on, Michael. Are you telling me that's actually against the law?'

'I'm afraid so, Jeff,' he says.

So there you have our great British legal system: a man who tries to protect his closest friends from financial ruin is locked up alongside robbers, murderers and perjurers. I only hope the Home Secretary, Mr David Blunkett, is reading this right now, or that someone is reading it to him. To be honest, I'm not sure that we're actually bothering with a Braille version. If not he will probably have to wait for the audio book to come out, which might take a while, but when I finally get out of this hellhole and into the recording studio I will read this particular section in a very loud and angry voice:

Are you paying attention, Home Secretary? This man has done nothing wrong, and yet you are punishing him cruelly.

Michael goes on to tell me that he had to be moved from another wing because the other inmates were starting to ask him to pick stocks for their portfolios.

Did you get that Home Secretary? This elderly, innocent man is being forced to give financial advice to criminals!

He then shows me the scar running up his arm, where he was slashed with a lollipop which had been licked to a deadly point. He was attacked in the prison showers by a con whose pension fund had collapsed.

Now you listen here, Home Secretary: I know you to be a fair man, but this is all your fault. If this man dies in prison you will be guilty of murder, and you will rot in Hell, despite the admirable way you have overcome your handicap.

In spite of our mutual innocence, Michael and I chat on like a couple of old lags. I show him my own impressive scar, which not many people know about. It runs from my left ear along my jaw line, under my chin and back to my right ear.

'Now, do you know how I got that?' I ask.

'Facelift?' asks a surly young lag seated behind us. Prison humour.

'Tokyo Olympics,' I say. 'Nearly decapitated by my own hurdle. I was in a coma for two weeks, and didn't know I'd won the Silver until I woke up.'[18]

---

18. I would have got the Gold had it not been for the fact that the race was in metres instead of yards.

DAY 17

3:30 PM

As time wears on and word filters out that I am working under cover to expose the hard, dark underbelly of the prison system, more and more inmates drop by my cell to pass on their life stories so that I can record them in my diary. When I can, I try to offer helpful advice.

'This is getting a bit boring,' I say. 'Skip to the part where you were arrested.' Most are grateful for the editorial help; they know this is their one chance to share some of the most shameful episodes in their tragic lives with millions of people by means of a £1.5 million pound national newspaper serialisation. That is by no means the final figure by the way. Negotiations continue.

Slowly I am learning how things work inside.

Hamish (murder) comes by. I have invited him to speak to me in the strictest confidence about being a 'grass', or someone who informs on other prisoners in return for favours from the guards and reduced sentence time. He seems reluctant to speak, but I'm relying on him for information about the system, and the other inmates. At times he talks in such a whisper that I have to ask him to speak up so I can write his words down exactly. It doesn't help that he has a thick Glaswegian accent and a deep scar across his lower lip. I show him my own ear-to-ear scar, the one I got in the Paris–Dakar rally. I think it cheers him up a little.

DAY 18

5:55 AM

Slept surprisingly well. Dawn filters through my little barred window. Write for two hours.

9:00 AM

Breakfast (my new favourite, Tango and Pringles – I almost prefer it to the Eggs Florentine at the Savoy).

10:00 AM

Still avoiding the exercise yard as a precaution. For a naturally energetic person like myself, this is the ultimate torture. Nothing to do but read, write and eat Kit Kats, and still I'm losing weight. Down to 186 at last weigh-in.

11:20 AM

Post. The deluge of letters is finally beginning to tail off slightly, but the parcels keep on coming: no fewer than 17 bibles to sign today! At this rate Hellmarsh is going to need a bigger library!

2:17 PM

Another surprise visit from the prison governor, Ms Gregory. She is doing something different with her hair, which is much more flattering to her face. In fact she is really quite attractive. She tells me she has high hopes of getting me transferred to Hell-Next-The-Sea, one of Britain's most notorious open prisons, as soon as possible, but unfortunately she is still waiting for my D-cat status to be restored. With a perfect deadpan expression she asks if I will kindly refrain from going berserk in the Education wing until then. Oh dear – I'm actually beginning to find this bleak prison humour quite amusing. I laugh heartily, and she summons the guard.

DAY 19

5:23 AM

The earliest I've been up yet. The light of dawn has not even begun to filter through my little barred window.

9:30 AM

Another big Sunday breakfast (eggs, beans, crisps, Tango, 2 Milky Bars). Have I really been here that long?

11:00 AM

This week the guard on duty spots my light at once, and I am escorted to the C of E service in plenty of time. The number of worshippers attending appears to be down slightly, perhaps because of my absence last week. I notice the vicar is still wearing the same grubby coat and dog-collar he had on two weeks ago. He'll never make bishop dressing like that. For the sermon I take as my text The Eleventh Commandment, which is, as all good Christians know, 'Thou Shall Not Get Caught'. Full house or no, I think it's safe to say that everyone present has violated this commandment at least once.

1:18 PM

The vicar drops by, still in the same shabby coat and dog-collar he was wearing at chapel, to say that the Bibles I've donated are leaving the library almost as soon as they come in.

'I'm glad to be of help,' I say.

'The trouble is, they're not being returned. They're being stolen.'

'That'll be the autographs, I expect,' I say. 'Not to worry. I've got a dozen more signed bibles in this box. You can take them now if you like. At this rate we'll soon have two bibles for every lag in Hellmarsh.'

2:30 PM

The guard arrives to tell me I have a visitor. It's the very person I've been longing to see: my solicitor Alex, who in addition to being my solicitor is almost as close a friend to me as Mary is in addition to being my wife. He warns me that he has bad news. Emma Nicholson MP has demanded a police investigation into the Kurdish appeal, which means my C-cat status will probably not be changed.

'I know a man who can have her bumped off,' I say. I'm not sure he realises I am joking. I am.

4:00 PM

I am summoned to see the governor, Ms Gregory. Trousers suit her. Unfortunately she confirms the worst: my C-cat classification will remain indefinitely. She assures me however, that she is extremely keen to get shot of me, so I will be transferred to Wayhell Prison in Norfolk, where the regime is slightly more relaxed that in Hellmarsh, but only slightly. From there I may be transferred to an open prison when I become category D again. I am to leave in two days.

5:35 PM

I am stunned, to say the least. It appears that I will be serving my sentence in at least three different prisons, which means that my bestselling prison diary will now have to take the form of a trilogy rather than the form which has just two books in it. I will need to contact my publishers and my agent immediately.

DAY 20

5:30 AM

Light filtering little barred window: start write. Not much time left. Just two days finish diary. No breakfast me.

11:00 AM

Exercise.

A brisk, bracing stroll around the exercise yard gives me a chance to say good-bye to a few old friends. I break the news of my imminent transfer to Daryl (murder, fuck), Bob (drugs, bible) and Ron (burglary, can have Emma Nicholson killed), who are all understandably upset. I also run into Hamish (murder, grass), who says he has had second thoughts about me using his real name in my diary. In three weeks he is the only person who has made that request. 'Don't worry, Frederick,' I shout back without missing a beat, 'your secret is safe with me!' And Frederick henceforth he shall be.

The 'Escape Committee' has proved itself to be a group more interested in talk than action. If they had hoped that the details of their daring escape would turn up in either my searingly truthful prison diary or my galloping prison-break thriller, then their hopes were to prove in vain. I tell them I am being transferred. They seem unsure as to how to react.

'Hope to see you on the outside,' I say to their leader, 'if you ever make it.'

'Actually, I'm getting out next week,' he replies. I can't help but admire his foolish, self-delusional courage. He reminds me of a young me.

'Well, good luck,' I say. 'And don't breathe a word of your plans to that snitch Frederick.'[19]

12:30 PM

Dinner (Cup a Soup, Kit Kat, 6 fairy cakes, Lilt). I hope the food is as good in Wayhell.

2:00 PM

Writing and more writing.

---

19. Hamish.

5:40 PM

A last 'Tea' (Coco Pops, Pringles, remainder of Kit Kats (8), half-packet jelly babies, 'Snickers').

8:00 PM

Association has been cancelled due to another 'lockdown' situation. Large quantities of drugs are coming into the prison, but the authorities have no idea how. Random searches have been instituted. My cell was among the first to be torn apart. Oh well: I guess I've said most of my good-byes.

My last night 'banged up' in Hellmarsh. I hardly dare believe it.

DAY 21

5:54 AM

For the last time the dawn light filters through my little barred window. I have already packed my few things neatly in the bin liner provided.

I can feel my Hellmarsh prison diary bringing itself to a natural conclusion. There is just time to tie up a few narrative loose ends. Davy (going equipped, former cellmate), who during my time here became not just my cellmate, but also one of my closest friends in the world, left prison nearly a week ago. I forgot to mention it at the time because of the Gillian Shepherd dream.

Little Steve, who came to my creative writing class mired in illiteracy, can now read a fair bit, partly because of my help and partly because he was actually a composite of several illiterate inmates I had met, one of whom, it turns out, can actually read perfectly well.

I also understand that the ongoing stress of Frederick's role as a Hellmarsh 'grass' has landed him in the prison medical ward with a case of severe stomach wounds. Several of the cons from my wing tell me he was already unconscious when they found him in the prison shower. Very sad.

8:02 AM

The key turns in the lock. The door opens. I walk down the corridor for the last time, waving and yelling to my friends as I go: 'So long, Daryl! (murder, fuck)'; 'Take care, Bob (drugs, bible) – may the Force of God be with you!'; 'Good-bye, Ron! (burglary, Emma Nicholson), don't forget to make it look like an accident!'

As the steel door at the end of the corridor clangs shut behind me for the final time, I have mixed feelings. In three weeks I learned so much about Hellmarsh, its ways and its inmates, and yet I never had a chance to use the pool. Perhaps one day I will return to it in better circumstances, perhaps – who knows? – as HM inspector of prisons. Then I will test that pool thoroughly.

For now, however, I am happy to be stepping into the bright yellow sunshine, and into the back of a gleaming white van. Soon I will be beyond Hellmarsh's gates forever, speeding down the open road toward another prison. And as soon as I get there I will sit down in my new cell, take out my A4 pad and write this last bit.

THE END

TO ORDER FURTHER COPIES

Not the Archer Prison Diary by Tim Dowling
ISBN 0-091-89239-2 £3.99

FREE POST AND PACKING
Overseas customers allow £2.00 per paperback

BY PHONE: 01624 677237

BY POST: Random House Books
C/o Bookpost, PO Box 29, Douglas
Isle of Man, IM99 1BQ

BY FAX: 01624 670923

BY EMAIL: bookshop@enterprise.net

Cheques (payable to Bookpost) and credit cards accepted

Prices and availability subject to change without notice.
Allow 28 days for delivery.
When placing your order, please mention if you do not wish to receive any additional information.

www.randomhouse.co.uk